Home Evenings
for Empty Nesters

Home Evenings for *Empty Nesters*

Activities to Strengthen the Later Years of Marriage

Alison Palmer

WALNUT SPRINGS PRESS

Cover design by Tracy Anderson

ISBN: 978-1-59992-979-8

Printed in the United States of America

Contents

Appreciation

Read

Doctrine and Covenants 46:9–26

Discuss

Marriage is a give-and-take relationship where we balance our different gifts and abilities to benefit both spouses and strengthen our eternal bond. On a daily basis, do you prayerfully seek to recognize and express your best gifts and to see and appreciate your partner's? How does this increase your unity as a couple, as opposed to when you concentrate on traits you feel he or she is lacking?

How does identifying your gifts, building on them, and coordinating them with your husband's or wife's gifts enhance the relationship and bless everyone you know, especially your children and grandchildren?

Recall a time in your marriage where your differences have caused contention. How was this overcome? How has honoring your unique qualities helped you appreciate each other more over the years?

Share and discuss the qualities you most appreciate about each other. What makes your spouse unique and special to you? How do your different talents and challenges balance each other out?

Activity

Play "A: I Adore You," using the letters from a Scrabble game. Take turns drawing a random letter and coming up with a word starting with that letter that describes your mate.

Treat

Make a snack mix to represent how your talents, gifts, and interests mix with your spouse's in a perfect medley.

Beatitudes

Read

Matthew 5:1–10

Discuss

What were the circumstances surrounding Jesus Christ's delivery of the Sermon on the Mount? What did He hope to teach and accomplish with this particular sermon?

Take time to discuss each verse of the Beatitudes. Give examples of how you have tried to live each principle, and consider sharing an experience where you could have done better.

For each of the virtues mentioned in the Beatitudes, find a story in the scriptures where someone displays the virtue.

Going forward, how can you more fully incorporate the principles of the Beatitudes into your life? Why is it essential for a disciple of Christ to possess and strengthen these character traits? How can you encourage your children and grandchildren to develop these traits?

To help transform the spirit of your home and strengthen your marriage, make a goal to focus each week on a different virtue from the Beatitudes.

Activity

Put the ingredients for homemade ice cream in a Mason jar. Place the jar inside a #10 can and layer ice and rock salt around the jar. Tightly seal the can and roll it back and forth between you and your spouse as you memorize and practice the scripture verses from the lesson. Keep rolling the can for about 10 minutes, then open the lid to see if your ice cream is ready. If not, roll for another 10 minutes. If it still hasn't reached the desired constancy, a few minutes in the freezer will finish the process for you.

Treat

Add some toppings to your ice cream, or eat it plain. Enjoy!

Book of Mormon

Watch or Read

"Safety for the Soul," Elder Jeffrey R. Holland, October 2009 general conference (video and text available on lds.org)

Discuss

Discuss the things that belong at the center of your life. How do these often get displaced by other concerns? How can we re-establish our priorities according to our faith and beliefs?

Why does Elder Holland call the Book of Mormon a "powerful keystone" that can keep our testimonies strong and properly centered? Read and review at least one of the stories he shares in his talk. How has it helped your testimony grow?

Elder Holland refers to the Book of Mormon as a safe harbor of love, healing, help, and hope. Find and discuss additional Book of Mormon stories that portray each of these gifts. Share your thoughts and feelings with each other.

Describe your experience of receiving a testimony of the Book of Mormon, or a time when it was strengthened. Then listen reverently as your spouse shares a testimony-building experience of his or her own.

Activity

In a new copy of the Book of Mormon, write your testimonies, gearing them specifically toward your posterity.

Treat

"Golden plate" grilled cheese sandwiches

Charity

Read

1 Corinthians 13

Discuss

List the ways the Apostle Paul describes charity in this portion of his epistle to the Corinthians. What other words or examples would you add to the list from experiences in your own lives?

How does understanding the Savior's love for you personally, and for all of mankind, increase your desire to feel this same kind of love for others? We are counseled by the prophet Moroni to "pray unto the Father with all the energy of [our] hearts, that [we] might receive this love" (see Moroni 7:48). Once we have received the gift of charity, how can we let it change our hearts and guide our daily actions?

Review the different aspects of charity and how each can enrich and strengthen a marriage. In what ways should charity guide the way you treat each other?

Activity

Trace each other's shadow silhouettes and mount them on contrasting paper. On the back, list the qualities of charity you see in your mate.

Treat

Cream puffs

Choices

Watch or Read

"LDS Women Are Incredible!" Elder Quentin L. Cook, April 2011 general conference (video and text available on lds.org)

Discuss

Do you think the young woman in Elder Cook's story specially prepared her purse for the dance just in case she lost it, so the items inside would make her look good to others? How do you think her value of these items, and what they represented, might have been evident to others even if they never looked inside her purse?

Next, talk about the importance of the pioneer spirit in the early decades of the restored Church. Why did people all over the world decide to gather with the Saints in the United States, and to cross the plains to the West? Did they have room to take along possessions they thought would impress the other Saints or increase their own standing? In most cases, they only had space to bring items essential to survival.

Recall a move of your own. How did you decide what to leave and what to take?

Elder Cook's message focuses on the great strength of women in the Church, both among the pioneers and the modern Saints. What strengths does he point out in their character? How are these traits evident in what matters most to them? What have these women chosen to pack in their handcarts and purses? Do you think these choices required any sacrifices?

Being a righteous person usually has more to do with qualities that aren't always obvious on the outside—such as compassion, creativity, and faith—than in traits easily seen by a casual observer. Just as the leaders in the story could not tell which young woman the purse belonged to until they opened it, the best parts of a person, his or her God-given gifts and talents, often take time and effort to discover.

Activity

Each of you write or type up a story from your life of how you made a certain choice. Explain the consequences, good or bad, that followed. Tell what you would have done differently, if anything, if you had known what you know now. Mail or email the story to each of your grandchildren. If you don't have grandchildren yet, send the story to another young person you know well, such as a niece or nephew.

Treat

Black Forest cake

Christ-Centered Lives

Read

2 Nephi 25:19–29

Discuss

Share favorite stories from Jesus Christ's life and discuss some of His traits. What have you learned as you try to live more like He did during mortality?

Why do you think so many people wanted to be near the Savior during His earthly ministry? Did they all understand who He was and what He could do for them?

Talk about the ways you and your spouse are currently striving to bring the Lord into your lives and home. Discuss how each of you try to center your day on Him. In what ways do you work on this process as a couple?

How does Heavenly Father view us and our abilities? Will He only grant the righteous desires of people who live the gospel perfectly?

Part of the focus of these verses was to remind the Nephites to look forward to Christ's birth. What signs were given of His coming? How were the shepherds, Wisemen, and others directed in their search for Him? The counsel given to the Nephites applies to each of us today. The more we talk of, rejoice in, preach of, and write of Christ, the more we will look forward to the time when He will return to earth to rule and reign.

Activity

Seeking Jesus Scripture Hunt: Each of you open your scriptures to a random spot (no cheating!) and count the number of times a name or title for Jesus Christ is given on the open pages. The spouse with the highest number wins each round.

Treat

Cream-filled pastries

Commandments

Watch or Read

"When the Lord Commands," Elder Bruce A. Carlson, April 2010 general conference (video and text available on lds.org)

Discuss

Most rules and directions need to be followed precisely in order to achieve the desired results. In general terms, discuss the things that might keep us from exactly obeying the Lord's commandments.

Read 1 Nephi 17:8–9 and Ether 2:16. Discuss how both groups of people had to build ships to travel to a land of promise. Nephi's ship and the Jaredite barges were built according to the Lord's instructions, rather than according to how other ships were normally constructed in those days. Discuss how many of the things the Lord commands us to do are different from the world's way of doing things.

Talk about the three excuses identified by Elder Carlson. Then discuss situations that might occur in the world today that would be comparable to those faced by Nephi's family and the Jaredites. What other scriptural and modern comparisons can you think of that follow this theme?

After you cover all three areas, each of you write down one commandment. It can be anything we've been asked to do—whatever comes to mind. Discuss which of Elder Carlson's excuses someone might use in order to justify not keeping the commandment. Next, come up with answers or counsel that could be given to such a person. Discuss the benefits and blessings of following the Lord's commandment in each situation.

How do the commandments and our covenants help us understand the Lord's will for us as individuals and as a couple?

Activity

Visit a lake or other body of water and take a walk along the shoreline.

Treat

Have you ever prepared a meal or treat and left out an important ingredient? Remake that meal or treat, being sure to follow the recipe exactly.

Communication

Watch or Read

"Language: A Divine Way of Communicating," Elder Charles Didier, October 1979 general conference (video and text available on lds.org)

Discuss

"Consider words, sentences, and languages. What are they? How do they affect us, our families, and our Heavenly Father?" After Elder Didier said this, he went on to declare that language is divine. In what ways is it divine? How can words lift us? Recall a time when someone's words have touched just the right chord within your heart.

How easy is it to misunderstand what someone is saying? In a world where few listen to understand instead of respond or defend, what strategies can you practice to help your communication as a couple be mutually beneficial? How does involving the Lord in our communications, through prayer and following the Spirit, help us to expand our perceptions to see those around us as He sees them?

Discuss ways you and your spouse can communicate with more love. For instance, effective communication often means staying in the present tense, rather than bringing up past wrongs. Arguing about potholes on a different road from the one you are currently traveling is not loving or productive. Don't bring up past problems, or current but separate problems, when trying to deal with an obstacle.

Activity

Learn to create simple origami figures. Write love notes to each other, fold them in to origami shapes, and hide them all over the house for your spouse to find at random times during the coming week.

Treat

Alphabet soup

Compassion

Watch or Read

"Compassion," President Thomas S. Monson, April 2004 general conference (video and text available on lds.org)

Discuss

After reviewing the examples of compassion described by President Monson, discuss further examples you have witnessed in your own life. Where have you observed the Savior's compassionate touch in the world around you?

Which words does President Monson use to describe compassion?

How does the Savior provide our best examples of compassion?

What goals can we set to help us become more compassionate?

There are so many opportunities for doing good. As President Monson declared: "These accounts pertain to the Redeemer of the world. Can there actually occur in my own life, on my own Jericho road, such a treasured experience?"

Jesus Christ's eyes were open to people that others refused to see. His heart found good in everyone, and He taught us to love as He did. It takes just three things to begin to teach someone this same love: loving eyes and ears, loving hearts, and loving examples.

As you begin to open your eyes on your personal Jericho Road, your heart will grow. When your return help for hurt as Joseph in Egypt did, your compassion will increase. As you join hands with those who are hurting in your community, you will share the Savior's compassion with the world.

Activity

Go out to eat and open your heart to seek an opportunity to pay for someone else's meal as well.

Treat

Dinner—and a full heart

Consequences

Watch or Read

"Come unto Me with Full Purpose of Heart, and I Shall Heal You," Elder Patrick Kearon, October 2010 general conference (video and text available on lds.org)

Discuss

Talk about rules you had in your family over the years. Which ones were constant? Did all family members feel the rules were fair? Even though there are times when breaking a rule doesn't seem to cause any harm, the potential danger is there. Ignoring it once may lead us to ignore it more often until something bad does happen.

Review Elder Kearon's story about taking a walk in the desert without proper footwear. Did he understand the importance of the rule? Why did he think it would be okay to break it?

Next, discuss some of the commandments and why keeping them is so critical. How do they help protect us? Remember that consequences are not always obvious or severely damaging, but each time we break a commandment, we place ourselves in a position where the Holy Ghost cannot be our companion, and we open doorways to problems that could have been easily avoided. Reflect on a time when you felt the negative consequences of not keeping a commandment, and follow up by describing the blessings you have received from choosing to follow a certain commandment.

Review the story of the Anti-Nephi-Lehis—their rebellion and repentance. What if the people had locked the weapons in a trunk "just in case they needed them"? It took faith for the people to soften their hearts and turn them over to the Savior for healing. There could be no justifications or excuses. Discuss the power of the Atonement when we repent. Spend some time pondering whether there are portions of your own hearts that have been held back and need to be released.

Activity

Wearing proper shoes, go for a walk.

Treat

Scones with prickly-pear jam

Courage

Read

Alma 17:9–11

Discuss

Life is full of difficult journeys, as well as wonderful joys. Discuss the fact that true courage is not something that can be physically held, nor is it something someone else can give you. Just like faith, courage is a gift from God that comes when you put forth effort.

Discuss the methods the sons of Mosiah used to build up their courage as they faced a difficult task. What problems did they encounter, and what joys did they receive? What difference do you think it made that they were all united in the same goals and pleading for the same blessings from their Heavenly Father?

What areas of your own lives require the most courage right now? How do these same methods of supplication provide us with a measure of the Spirit as our own need arises?

Do we pray daily for the courage to strengthen our spirituality, lift our partner, and be an example of love and testimony? How do we seek out the blessing of being the Lord's instrument?

Recall a time when turning toward Heavenly Father and increasing your spirituality has led to an increased measure of courage and comfort in a difficult situation. How can the things you've learned from these past experiences provide renewed courage during future trials?

Activity

Step outside your comfort zone and support each other in trying something new, such as dancing, painting, or learning a new language.

Treat

Lemonade ("When life gives you lemons . . .")

Decision Making

Read

Philippians 4: 6–13

Discuss

How does the peace of God differ from man's version of peace and happiness?

Are the paths we find ourselves on always trouble-free and straight? What determines our reaction to the obstacles we encounter?

Where do we turn when we need a different perspective? What gentle urgings have you received regarding how to care for yourself and your spouse? What difference does our attitude make in this process?

Examine your own motives for service in the gospel and with your extended family. Which aspects of your life can you give up in order to have greater concern for others?

Discuss the methods these verses suggest for making hard decisions. How does the gospel and our relationship with the Savior lend us strength in difficult times?

How can our ability to focus on the good in our lives help us make decisions with the right spirit?

How do these verses compare to the thirteenth article of faith?

Activity

Take a drive to get some ice cream, counting how many stop signs you pass. Use that number as a daily goal for yourself to notice the good around you and make choices that emphasize that good.

Treat

Ice cream

Disagreements

Read

Ephesians 4:25–32

Discuss

Is there a place for arguments in marriage? Why or why not? While spouses sometimes disagree, it is important that we don't speak angry words, whether or not we purposely intend to hurt each other.

What harm can come to a relationship when unkind words are spoken and then allowed to fester?

What does the act of arguing steal from the marriage covenant, and how can it be restored?

Is there value in placing blame? How does blame differ from expressing your own feelings about a situation?

What strategies can be used to put away anger for kindness, acknowledge different perspectives, and see both sides of the story?

How has the spirit of your home changed over the years, based on your ability and your companion's ability to find kind and productive ways to express emotions and talk out differences?

Activity

Have a word war. Take a few quiet minutes where each of you think of a couple of times when you felt angry at or hurt by your spouse. Silently express these emotions on 8½" by 11" sheets of paper. Wad the sheets into balls and toss them at each other until the last of the hurtful feelings have dispelled. Then hold a small campfire for these old griefs and put them to rest permanently.

Treat

Roast s'mores over your campfire.

Diversity

Read

1 Corinthians 12

Discuss

Why is there such diversity in the spiritual gifts Heavenly Father gives to His children? Are all the gifts He can bestow listed in these verses? What other things might be added to the list, and what would be the purpose of each in edifying others and lifting them toward Christ?

How does this example of diversity with unity of purpose apply to our families, our wards, our communities, and so on? How can we apply the Apostle Paul's teachings within our own circles to better contribute to the good of the whole and appreciate the unique contributions of others?

When arguments become emotionally charged it can be difficult to remember to be open-minded, respect different perspectives, and appreciate both sides of a situation. How does acknowledging our differences as individuals and defining united goals for your family help this process? How do we develop open communication that allows both parties to feel comfortable expressing opinions and knowing that the other party will respect and try to understand those opinions?

Activity

Play "Name that Movie Quote." Take turns stating a quote from a favorite movie to see if your spouse can guess the title or continue the quote.

Treat

Gingerbread men decorated with unique personalities

Example

Read

2 Corinthians 3:2–6

Discuss

How do we act as a testament for the things written in our hearts?

How many different ways does the Apostle Paul express God's ability to comfort us during our trials and other times of trouble?

How does our personal testimony affect how we face trials? What do the examples around us teach us about facing our own trials?

Recall someone from your youth who valued you and helped you become a better person. How can you similarly help the youth around you—especially your posterity?

Have you known someone who seemed to do everything right, but left you with a feeling that all was not right with his or her spirit? How about the individual whose life seems to regularly take difficult turns, yet the person's soul emanates peace? What seems to make the difference?

Why do these scriptures appear to indicate that our spirit and our righteous happiness are a greater testimony than statements of faith or strict adherence to laws that can be seen by others? Is there a place for compromise between strict obedience and joyful obedience? How does increased spirituality lead to a greater understanding of personal journeys and differences?

Activity

Volunteer to help chaperone a dance, temple trip, or other youth activity.

Treat

Work together to create a treat from the example in a cooking video.

Faith

Watch or Read

"Developing Faith," Elder A. Theodore Tuttle, October 1986 (video and text available on lds.org)

Discuss

Has the Lord ever asked you to do something you didn't think you were capable of? What happened when you allowed Him to assist you with the task?

Relate a story of faith from your side of the family tree. Then listen as your spouse tells a faith-filled story from one of his or her ancestors. Have these memories been shared with the younger generations of your family? If not, make a plan to share them in the near future.

How do trials strengthen our faith and make the rewards for acting on our beliefs even more sweet? How have you tried to instill such faith in your children and grandchildren, or your nieces and nephews? What have they, in return, taught you about this powerful concept?

Think of your personal testimony. Where did your faith begin, and how did it grow? What portions of your testimony were hard won? Do you feel you are truly converted, so that you act daily on what you know to be true? Is there an area you still struggle with where you could apply the principles discussed in Elder Tuttle's talk in order to establish firmer roots of faith in your own life?

Activity

Try building a model ship together.

Treat

What was the "manna" of your early years of marriage? Have it again tonight.

Family History

Watch or Read

"The Hearts of the Children Shall Turn," Elder David A. Bednar, October 2011 general conference (video and text available at lds.org)

Discuss

Talk about your experiences with family history. Are you active genealogists or not? What influences have gone into your choices and the amount of time and energy you spend seeking out your own ancestors? What factors have gone into determining how close you feel to different relatives in your family?

Begin a discussion about Elijah:

- Who was he?
- What was the goal of his mortal ministry?
- Which special keys did he pass down to Joseph Smith during the Restoration?
- How do these keys pertain to the ordinances of the temple?

Talk about the importance of eternal families. Just as there are activities we use to strengthen the family within the home (such as family prayer, scripture study, and family home evening), there are activities we can use to become closer to those who aren't nearby, such as children and grandchildren who live in another city or state or country.

Think of ways you and your spouse can reach out and become closer to extended relatives who are still living. Then, expand the discussion to talk about ways family history can help bring that same type of closeness to family members who have previously died, or those who will live after we are gone from the earth.

Activity

Have someone teach you how to use a video communication program (such as Skype or FaceTime) so you can keep in touch with your family members who live far away.

Treat

Heart-shaped pancakes

Family Time

Watch or Read

"A Table Encircled with Love," Elder LeGrand R. Curtis, April 1995 general conference (video and text available at lds.org)

Discuss

One of the greatest gifts we have received in this mortal life is our family. As family members, we learn to work together and to encourage and help each other qualify to return to Heavenly Father. When we do this, we are working to become a forever family. As every member of the family shares all of their best qualities, a happy family results.

Read the following scriptures and identify the building block mentioned that will help you work to build strong families.

- 3 Nephi 18:21 (prayer)
- 2 Nephi 4:15 (scriptures)
- 3 Nephi 22:13 (family home evening and gospel discussions)

Recall your favorite memories of your younger family around the dinner table. Now think about similar times with your grown children or your grandchildren. What effort did it require on your part to make these moments happen? While you might not have always felt the effort was worth the results, could you see the benefits as the months and years went by?

Where possible, come up with a plan that will allow you to occasionally invite your children and grandchildren into your home for a special family home evening. Prayerfully consider the memories you would like them to take away from such experiences.

Activity

Look through family pictures together and share a favorite memory with each other of a time you were together as a family. Take a moment to discuss the blessings each person brings to the family.

Treat

Heart-shaped sugar cookies decorated with words of love for each other

Fear

Read

Psalms 46:1–11

Discuss

Share some childhood fears with each other. How did you overcome them? As an adult, what fears and anxieties do you face?

What tools are available to us, as members of the Lord's true Church, to help counter our fears?

Why doesn't God always intercede when we face times of stress and fear? Does He understand our needs and concerns during such times?

How does the temple act as a buffer against our fears?

Compare the number of times fear is mentioned in the scriptures, compared to peace. In what contexts is peace spoken of? What about fear? How can faith displace fear?

Activity

Turn off your phones, as well as any music or television, then snuggle quietly together for fifteen minutes.

Treat

Molten lava cake

Forget Me Not

Watch or Read

"Forget Me Not," President Dieter F. Uchtdorf, October 2011 general conference (video and text available on lds.org)

Discuss

Identify, and describe in a much detail as you can, a woman each of you admire. Are the things you first noticed about her large or small? What about later on in your acquaintance? Are these things everyone would notice about that person, or things that might be harder for some to see?

Review the five things President Uchtdorf said we should never forget.

- First, forget not to be patient with yourself.
- Second, forget not the difference between a good sacrifice and a foolish sacrifice.
- Third, forget not to be happy now.

- Fourth, forget not the "why" of the gospel.
- Fifth, forget not that the Lord loves you.

Discuss why you think President Uchtdorf addressed this subject with the women of the Church. One of the greatest blessings Heavenly Father has given to women is the ability to love and nurture those around them. This often includes very small and simple things that are easy to overlook. Women, especially those who lose themselves in the service of others, can feel just as small and insignificant as the tiny forget-me-not did. The women in our lives, and all children of God, need to remember that Heavenly Father loves them for who they are inside and for every good thing they do, whether large and small.

Go back through the five items once more. This time, spend a few moments pulling thoughts from the talk, and from your own family experiences, that could be used as examples of ways to remember these things.

Activity

Learn to make flowers out of paper or other recycled material.

Treat

Chocolate bars

Forgiveness

Read

1 Nephi 7:16–21

Discuss

We are told we must be forgiving if we want to be forgiven. No one ever said this was easy. Nor is it graded on a curve where forgiveness is not required when the sin is grave and cuts deeply.

What does it take to soften a heart?

What is the power of prayer in situations where trials of the heart are so very heavy?

In all honesty, discuss what types of prayers each of you might have uttered if you had found yourself in Nephi's situation. Where did his strength to pray come from?

Holding grudges and nursing old pain creates turmoil in our soul. Has there been a time in your life when you have needed to forgive another? How did you do so? Record your feelings both before and after you frankly forgave. Perhaps you still need to make a plan toward forgiveness. What would the Lord have you do to accomplish this?

What has the power of forgiveness contributed to the strength of your marriage?

Activity

Build a playing-card castle together. How many tries does it take to figure out the best method for making progress?

Treat

Licorice ropes

Friendship

Watch or Read

"What is a Friend?" Elder Marvin J. Ashton, October 1972 general conference (video and text available on lds.org)

Discuss

Talk about why friendship is a fundamental Christian principle.

How do friendship needs with a spouse differ from those with others? How are our needs for friendship and camaraderie met by different people?

In addition to your relationship with your spouse, which friendships hold the most value for you? Why?

What does our effort to develop and maintain different types of uplifting relationships ultimately say about our love of the Savior?

How can you strengthen the bonds of friendship with your husband or wife?

Activity

Find old pictures of childhood friends. Reminisce about these friends and write down some stories to include, along with the photos, in your personal histories.

Treat

Amish friendship bread

God's Love

Read

John 3:14–17

Discuss

Share and review your favorite conference talks or other material about God's love for His children. His love for us, and for the world, can feel both vast and personal. After you and your spouse discuss some of what others have had to say on the subject, share your own experiences with each other.

When have you felt overwhelmed by all of Heavenly Father's blessings in your life? What did this lead you to do? Did it make you want to go out and serve others and share your blessings?

What are your most treasured moments when the Holy Ghost helped you understand the intimate nature of God's love?

How has your understanding of God's love for you affected your own thoughts and feelings about yourself?

When you are able to recognize Heavenly Father's love for you, how does it change your view of those around you? How does it change your attitude toward your spouse?

What happens when life is dark and we have forgotten the beautiful touch of God's love in our lives? When we allow things into our lives that dim our view of His love, does this mean He has abandoned us? What can we do to open our eyes to the many different ways Heavenly Father reaches out to touch and bless our lives every day?

Activity

Visit a botanical garden and observe both nature and people.

Treat

Nibble on a few conversation hearts as you come up with phrases you might see on them if they had been designed for you by Heavenly Father.

Gratitude

Watch or Read

"Gratitude," Elder Gordon T. Watts, October 1998 general conference (video and text available on lds.org)

Discuss

As you sit with your spouse, set a timer for two minutes. Each of you is to look around whatever area you are in and write down as many blessings as he or she can see. These may be tangible items, or memories associated with the items. When the time is up, compare your lists. How many different ways can you think of to express and show gratitude for your blessings?

How does Satan work to affect the way you view your blessings?

What happens in different aspects of our lives as we compare our situation with those of others?

Elder Watts suggests that gratitude can have "many faces." What faces have you seen gratitude wear?

In what ways do we fail to recognize our own blessings? How can our expressions of gratitude sometimes fall short of what they should be?

How does expressing gratitude for even what seems to be a small blessing enable us to see and receive even more blessings?

How can we learn to have gratitude and give sincere and meaningful thanks even in difficult times?

Activity

Visit a "pick your own" farm or orchard.

Treat

Hold a picnic with your some of your harvest.

Happiness

Watch or Read

"Happiness," Elder Jack H. Goaslind, April 1986 general conference (video and text available at lds.org)

Discuss

Talk about people you know who live life with joy and happiness. What traits do they have that you try to emulate? Have you expressed your appreciation to these friends for their examples?

How does the happiness offered through the gospel differ from the types of happiness often sought by those around us?

Discuss the following statement by Elder Goaslind: "Our yearnings for happiness were implanted in our hearts by Deity. They represent a kind of homesickness, for we have a residual memory of our premortal existence. They are also a foretaste of the fulness of joy that is promised to the faithful. We can expect with perfect faith that our Father will fulfill our innermost longings for joy."

What is the difference between sin, shortcomings, and adversity, and how can they affect a person's ability to feel happy? Are the feelings of dissatisfaction and unhappiness based in the Spirit quietly nudging us to do and be better, or other sources that would like to see us discouraged and beaten down by our trials?

Share and describe a time when you have felt the most joyful, alive, or at peace with life. What do you do to preserve these types of memories?

Activity

Purchase and begin personal gratitude journals. Each night, record something you are grateful for about the day that is ending. No complaints allowed.

Treat

Warm biscuits and preserves

Healing

Read

Psalms 147:1–5

Discuss

Find a broken object in your home. It can be as simple as a worn sock, or a shirt that is missing a button, or more complicated, like a broken lamp or a leaking inner tube for a bicycle tire. Discuss how the item came to need repair, and determine how you will fix it. Work together to carry out the solution.

Compare the repaired item to its original state and its broken one. Can you still tell the item has been broken? How well did the solution and repair work? Apply this to the Savior's Atonement and how it can repair and heal us.

An infant does not come to earth knowing how to do everything it needs to grow and survive. The baby receives help from those who love him or her. Even so, there will be times when things go wrong.

When the child learns to walk, it will take time, a number of falls, and sometimes cuts and bruises before he or she can stand tall and run and walk as Heavenly Father intended.

As we learn and grow, we may face times when our body or spirit is broken. With help from those who love us, and especially through the healing power of the Atonement, our lives can be repaired.

Share a moment when you understood the personal nature of Christ's love for you. How did you first come to understand that He knows your name and can heal your heart? Next, listen as your spouse shares such a moment from his or her life.

How has your marriage been an effort in learning and growing as Heavenly Father intended? At what points did you need to call on powers beyond your own in order to repair your relationship?

Activity

Go stargazing together. See how many constellations you can pick out, then create your own constellations that tell the story of your life and love.

Treat

Stained-glass cookies

Heritage

Watch or Read

"Generations Linked in Love," Elder Russell M. Nelson, April 2010 general conference (video and text available on lds.org)

Discuss

In what kinds of activities does your family engage to feel closer to family members both living and dead? Is there something more that could be done to reinforce those eternal bonds?

Heavenly Father has made provisions for all of His children to stay connected to Him and to each other. This is one reason we are commanded to return to the temple again and again. Each time we go, we open a way for someone who has passed on, so that he or she may attain the precious eternal blessings we enjoy.

Discuss how technological advances and a great increase in the number of temples have made it easier and more efficient to seek out and bind ourselves to our ancestors.

Understanding the importance of our own family relationships can help us realize how important we are to Heavenly Father. As we reach out to our family members, both living and deceased, we will feel a greater love for each other, for them, and for God.

Heavenly Father values our families and their ability to help us return us to His presence. What can you do as a family to show that you value each other as He does?

Activity

With your spouse, share stories about two or three ancestors you admire. Write a letter or email to your children or grandchildren, explaining what you have learned from these particular ancestors.

Treat

Make a favorite dessert recipe that has been passed through the generations of your family. Then enjoy the treat.

His Hands

Watch or Read

"You Are My Hands," President Dieter F. Uchtdorf, April 2010 general conference (video and text available on lds.org)

Discuss

Talk about the decisions each of us get to make about what our hands will do each day—comb our hair, fold the clothes, hold open the door for a stranger, shake the hand of a new friend, etc. Also discuss choices we could make that might not be good for us or our posterity. Think about the types of things we could do if we wanted to be the Savior's hands here on earth.

Write "You Are My Hands" on the top of a piece of paper. List key words you each remember from President Uchtdorf's talk down the left side of the page. Discuss each topic and brainstorm a list of possible actions our hands can do on behalf of Jesus Christ. List these on the right side of the paper.

During the discussion of the woman who compares herself to a $20 bill, talk about the part different hands have in deciding whether a dollar bill is kept nice. Is the true value accounted for by actions that can wear it out faster, such as wadding it up, tearing it, forgetting it, and letting it go through the washer?

How does that compare to the way we choose to treat individuals? Do our views and our actions contribute to how they view themselves? Does it change Heavenly Father's view of the individuals' worth? How about the way you treat your spouse? How would our actions change if we held everyone in that same value and respect?

Trace each other's hands on top of your lists. For a week, display the picture in a prominent place as a reminder of the importance of what we do with our hands.

Activity

Spend time working at the bishop's storehouse or a soup kitchen. Or make cookies for a neighbor or friend.

Treat

Canned peaches and cottage cheese

Honesty

Watch or Read

"I Believe in Being Honest and True," Sister Ann M. Dibb, April 2011 general conference (video and text available on lds.org)

Discuss

Using examples from Sister Dibb's talk, discuss the impact that even just two of the virtues in the thirteenth article of faith, being honest and true, can have on a person's life.

Discuss the following quote from *Jane Eyre,* by Charlotte Brontë: "I will respect myself. I will keep the law given by God. . . . Laws and principles are not for the times when there is no temptation: they are for moments such as this."

Review the thirteenth article of faith and talk about each of the virtues and attributes mentioned in it. Why do you think the Lord asks us to seek after such things? Have there been times when you have placed too much value on things that were not virtuous, lovely, of good report, or praiseworthy, but that instead were based on worldly standards? How did clinging to such objects or beliefs change your perception of what was most important in your life?

Choose one virtue you have put aside and make a goal to value and act on it more often.

Activity

Go geocaching (see geocaching.com). Or try your hand at using a metal detector.

Treat

Corn on the cob

Humility

Read

Matthew 18:1–14; watch or read "Become as a Little Child," Sister Jean A. Stevens, April 2011 general conference (video and text available on lds.org)

Discuss

The Savior declared that in order to enter into God's kingdom, we must become as little children and humble ourselves. Why is humility critical to our salvation, as well as to our happiness in this mortal life? How can you be more humble on a daily basis?

What lessons in humility have you learned from your children, your grandchildren, or your nieces and nephews?

In her conference address, Sister Stevens mentions several other positive traits of little children. How can we emulate those traits in our relationships, especially with Heavenly Father? Make a goal to pray to be more humble and teachable.

Activity

Share with each other your memories of your favorite toy, book, blanket, or other valued item from childhood. If you still have the item, show it to your spouse as you talk about it.

Treat

A classic food from your childhood or your spouse's

Intimacy

Watch or Read

"Nurturing Marriage," Elder Russell M. Nelson, April 2006 general conference (video and text available at lds.org)

Discuss

Talk about the reasons marriage is so important to Heavenly Father and, in contrast, so hated by the adversary.

Are there times when you let other priorities overwhelm the sacred calling we have to nurture and strengthen our family unit?

How do the ways you and your spouse express affection, and desire to receive it, differ between you? How are your desires similar? Do you regularly communicate with your husband or wife in regard to your feelings and preferences?

Review the two methods Elder Nelson suggests for strengthening marriage. How have these helped your relationship through the years, and how can they continue to be of use in your current stage of life?

Discuss the value and sacredness of intimacy in marriage. How can you both prepare for and create an environment of loving enjoyment when it comes to intimacy?

Activity

Put forth an extra effort to make your next intimate encounter, romantic, unique, and mindful of each other's needs and desires.

Treat

Wedding cake or other treat that was served at your wedding

Learning

Watch or Read

"Seek Learning: You Have a Work to Do," Sister Mary N. Cook, April 2012 general conference (video and text available at lds.org)

Discuss

How are we blessed when we take advantage of an opportunity to learn something new? What benefits come from pursuing education and secular learning? As we get older, we might see this type of learning as a chore or as something we don't have the energy to do. How can we change our perspective and come to enjoy learning new and interesting things? What will you do to make time for learning that brings you joy every day?

What benefits come from pursuing spiritual growth and learning? Can these pursuits be seen as burdensome as well? How do we change our attitudes and find the peace and joy of the gospel the Lord has in store for us?

Discuss why we need to continually grow in both secular and spiritual knowledge. Talk about the satisfaction and happiness that come as we learn and as we increase our abilities to serve the Lord, our families, and the world.

What is something you have always been grateful you learned how to do? What have you always wanted to learn, but haven't yet gotten to?

Activity

Find a free or low-cost community class to take together.

Treat

Snow cones

Listening

Read

James 1:1–23

Discuss

Much of this chapter of James focuses on asking questions to obtain greater understanding, learning to listen with real intent, and acting upon the things we hear. Discuss each of these aspects in turn, both as they pertain to the scriptures you read and as they apply to your own experiences in your lives and marriage.

What does it mean to be swift to hear? What is the difference between listening to respond, and the power of listening to understand? How does understanding the difference and learning to understand the other person's point of view have an effect on disagreements and escalating arguments in a marriage?

What is our responsibility toward our partner and our Heavenly Father for the things we have learned?

Activity

Attend a concert together and enjoy the different blends of voices and instruments used to create the music.

Treat

Elephant ears (fried, flattened dough topped with butter, sugar, and cinnamon)

Love for God

Watch or Read

"The Love of God," President Dieter F. Uchtdorf, October 2009 general conference (video and text available on lds.org)

Discuss

Talk about the different ways to describe a person (physical characteristics, habits, personality traits, etc.). Then discuss God's individual and intimate love for each of us. He has the ability to see into our souls, to know who we truly are and who we want to be. He knows us much better than even our family members do.

President Uchtdorf asks, "[O]f all the things we want to be known for, are there attributes above all others that should define us as members of His Church, even as disciples of Jesus Christ?" Review the implications of this question. What difference does your love for God make in your life? How do the things you love, seek, and do determine who you are and how others see you?

The more we find ways to love and serve God, making Him the center of our lives, the more our heart swells with increased love for Him. This love focuses our attention on pleasing Him by keeping the commandments and serving others. Acting on our love for God can change every aspect of our lives and make us into the disciples the Savior wants to be.

Activity

Take a course in CPR together.

Treat

Popcorn

Marriage Covenant

Watch or Read

"Families under Covenant," President Henry B. Eyring, April 2012 general conference (video and text available on lds.org)

Discuss

Review this quote by President Eyring: "There is nothing that has come or will come into your family as important as the sealing blessings. There is nothing more important than honoring the marriage and family covenants you have made or will make in the temples of God."

If you have been sealed to your spouse in the temple, talk specifically about the covenants the two of you made with God and each other at that time, and how you are trying to live up to those covenants. Review the role of the priesthood and priesthood keys in your marriage covenant, and how the sealing power builds an eternal family unit.

Review the four principles identified by President Eyring in this talk, which was given at general priesthood meeting:

- Gain a sure witness of the priesthood.
- Love your wife/mother.
- Love your entire family.
- Lead the family the Lord's way.

Based on these concepts, identify specific ways you and your husband or wife need to work harder to keep your marriage covenants. Discuss the difference between sacrifice and compromise. Why are both necessary? What role does the Holy Ghost play in your desires for righteousness?

Make a goal to never let your children and grandchildren doubt how much your marriage covenants mean to you.

Activity

Write a list of ten things you try to do regularly to show your spouse that you love him or her. Then write a list of ten ways your spouse makes you feel loved. Compare the lists.

Treat

What was your first meal or treat together as a married couple? Try to reproduce it.

Missionary Work

Read

Matthew 4:17–25

Discuss

Sometimes, sharing the gospel can seem frightening and difficult. It helps to remember that Heavenly Father is simply asking us to invite all of our family and friends to discover how the Savior's teachings can bless their lives. The gospel is something to celebrate, because it brings such joy when accepted and lived.

Recall and discuss different times in your lives when you shared the gospel with someone. What was his or her reaction? How did the experience strengthen your own faith?

Why did so many people follow Jesus Christ during the early part of his ministry? Were their motivations all the same? Talk about other people in the scriptures who were changed because they were willing to follow the Savior.

How do we become fishers of men? What things can we do to reflect Christ's love and attract people to His gospel? Are there things in our lives that should be left behind?

Activity

Go fishing or visit a nearby aquarium.

Treat

Fish and chips

Motes and Beams

Read

Matthew 7:1–5

Discuss

Why is it so much easier to see the faults in others rather than ourselves? What kinds of things can prevent us from seeing situations around us clearly? Is it ever acceptable or wise to point out a fault in another?

Discuss triggers in your own life that lead you to be more critical and judgmental of others. How do these judgments and grudges affect your marriage and other relationships?

When it comes to disagreements, what phrases and actions can lead to a constructive resolution of differences instead of unrighteous judgments and hurt feelings?

Recall a time when you or someone you love had a splinter. How much time and patience did it take to remove the hurtful item? How can we show greater kindness and patience to those who are in the process of trying to remove something from their lives, or change their hearts, in order to bring their lives into harmony with God's will? How can we show that same patience and love towards ourselves as we try to change?

Activity

Find an old piece of forgotten wood in your home or neighborhood and turn it into a decoration or useful object, such as a walking stick or a cheerful sign for your front door.

Treat

Try a new food that's a little outside your comfort zone.

Music

Watch or Read

"Worship through Music," Elder Dallin H. Oaks, October 1994 general conference (video and text available on lds.org)

Discuss

Review the message from the First Presidency on page ix of the hymnbook *(Hymns of The Church of Jesus Christ of Latter-day Saints).* If you don't have a copy of the hymnal in your home, you can access an electronic version on lds.org.

When we sing the hymns, Heavenly Father doesn't expect us to be the world's best vocalists. Rather, it is our attitude and effort that determine the quality of our worship. This can be observed among the Primary children. If the Spirit is strong, nothing is more rousing than hearing them enthusiastically sing "I Am a Child of God." Not every child will blend perfectly with his or her neighbor, hit all the notes with accuracy, or even sing all the correct words, yet the children clearly believe the words of the song, and singing it gives them great joy.

Review the tips Elder Oaks gives for making our own worship in song more meaningful. How do the hymns invite the Spirit into our meetings, homes, and lives? How can music enrich our testimonies?

What is your favorite hymn or Primary song? What about it speaks to you? If you had to choose one hymn in the morning to set the tone for your day, what would it be? What other types of music do you fill your day with? Why?

Activity

Sing or listen to your favorite hymns together.

Treat

Popcorn

My Shepherd

Read

Psalms 23:1–6

Discuss

Read the 23rd psalm, then listen to a musical performance of "The Lord Is My Shepherd." Talk about each verse separately—what it means to you and your spouse.

How does a shepherd care for and protect his sheep? How can this example help you and your spouse keep watch over your extended family and others within your sphere of influence?

Discuss how the Savior is our ultimate guide and mentor. Identify other people in your life who have acted as role models of spirituality, peace, comfort, leadership, and other traits mentioned in the psalm.

How does it bring you peace to know that Jesus Christ is the Good Shepherd? Decide to emulate His love as you seek out His sheep who are lost.

Activity

Watch the video "The Good Shepherd and Other Sheep I Have," on lds.org.

Treat

A favorite healthy salad

Overcoming Weaknesses

Watch or Read

"Broken Things to Mend," Elder Jeffrey R. Holland, April 2006 general conference (video and text available on lds.org)

Discuss

All of Heavenly Father's children are prone to commit sin and make mistakes, and we all have areas where we need to repent and improve. What is the difference between weakness and sin?

Discuss a few of your personal strengths and weaknesses. How do your strengths overlap and complement those of your spouse, and vice versa? How can the Atonement and the Savior's grace and power help us overcome our shortcomings?

Discuss the differences between thread and rope. Stress that when family members work together, their faith is strengthened. Discuss what you each feel are your greatest weaknesses and strengths as a couple.

How can you better learn to complement each other's strengths and work together to achieve your goals and support each other in times of trial?

Activity

Create a small mosaic together from paper, glass, or other recycled material. Or piece together a small section of a crazy or patchwork quilt from old clothes and scraps of material.

Treat

Cook a simple treat together that combines each of your favorite flavors.

Peace

Watch or Read

"Peace, Hope, and Direction," Sister Patricia P. Pinegar, October 1999 general conference (video and text available on lds.org)

Discuss

How does the gospel of Jesus Christ provide peace, hope, and direction for our lives?

Review the three things Sister Pinegar calls out as helpful in the pursuit of peace and hope.

Recall and discuss times in your own lives when you have had to put your complete trust in Heavenly Father's plan, exercise courageous obedience, or respond to the promptings of the Holy Ghost with faith and trust.

How does showing mindful awareness and gratitude for the blessings of peace, hope, and direction affect our ability to obtain greater peace?

Activity

Go fly kites together. Or listen to the testimony of a small child.

Treat

Homemade taffy

Prayer

Read

Mark 11:20–25

Discuss

Why is daily, heartfelt prayer so important? As we read in the Bible Dictionary: "Prayer is the act by which the will of the Father and the will of the child are brought into correspondence with each other. The object of prayer is not to change the will of God but to secure for ourselves and for others blessings that God is already willing to grant but that are made conditional on our asking for them."

Discuss your personal prayers. Are they a two-way communication with Heavenly Father, or do you simply thank Him for your blessings, ask for more, and say amen? Do you take time to listen quietly for inspiration during and after your prayer? Do you pray vocally whenever possible to help you focus on the conversation with your Heavenly Father? How can you let the Spirit teach you what to pray for?

Share your favorite scripture stories about prayer. Discuss the circumstances of each prayer, whether or not the prayer was answered right away, and the method by which it was answered. List the various ways you have had prayers answered. How does the Lord usually speak to you?

Is prayer alone enough as we seek personal revelation? What have many of the prophets said about meditating on spiritual matters? How can the act of fasting increase the power of our prayers?

Think of a time when someone has prayed for you and the Lord answered the prayer by blessing you. How did this build your faith?

Activity

Hold a special couple's prayer where each of you express gratitude, love, and respect for your spouse.

Treat

Homemade pretzels

Preparation

Read

3 Nephi 4:16–23

Discuss

What types of spiritual and physical sieges have you experienced during your lives? Looking back, what is one way you could have better prepared for those challenges? Have you made it a priority to strengthen your testimony and faithfully obey the commandments? How have the Lord and His prophets counseled us to prepare for life's challenges?

Share a moment when you thought something you desperately wanted was out of reach. What did you do to stretch yourself a little further? Did you reach your goal?

Discuss ways to prepare spiritually and physically for adversity. What efforts can you still make to become more self-sufficient? Discuss family goals and values, as well as ways to achieve and honor these goals in your daily lives.

Activity

Prepare or update a 72-hour kit for the two of you, or make a list of "must have" items for your food storage and a plan for gathering the items.

Ask your children or adult grandchildren what items they need to complete their 72-hour kits or their long-term food storage. Consider giving them some of these items as a Christmas gift.

Treat

Find the most unusual food item in your pantry—the one that always seems to get shoved aside and never eaten—and eat it.

Pride

Watch or Read

"Beware of Pride," President Ezra Taft Benson, April 1989 general conference (video and text available on lds.org)

Discuss

Talk about President Benson's definition of pride. How does it differ from the typical worldly definition?

Like any other sin, pride can sneak into our lives in small degrees. How has pride affected your life and your relationship with your Heavenly Father? What can be done to bring your will back in line with His?

Discuss President Benson's quote by C.S. Lewis on the nature of pride. How can you see the truth of Lewis's words in the world around us today?

Often, the prideful person feels that he or she is independent or above those around him, free from their restraints. In reality, how does pride give Satan power over us?

In what ways can pride affect a marriage? What can be done to prevent these sorts of problems?

Activity

Prayerfully decide on a person or family you will give a Book of Mormon to. Present it to them within the next three days.

Treat

Cream puffs

Priorities

Watch or Read

"A Time to Prepare," Elder Ian S. Ardern, October 2011 general conference (video and text available on lds.org)

Discuss

List the things that should be the highest priorities in your life. Do you try to put them first in your busy day, or are you always trying to fit them in? Are your priorities in line with the commandments of God?

Discuss the following quote from Elder Ardern: "Time is never for sale; time is a commodity that cannot, try as you may, be bought at any store for any price. Yet, when time is wisely used, its value is immeasurable."

What advice does Elder Ardern give for creating immeasurable value with our time? Discuss the place of family, service, prayer, and scripture study in our daily priorities. Conversely, what activities do we sometimes let crowd out the most important things?

How can you arrange your time so that those things with the most value are not overlooked or forgotten? Come up with ideas for keeping your priorities in mind. Forgo nonessential things that make you feel stressed and pressured for time. Remember that your Heavenly Father is mindful of your life and will help you in this endeavor.

Activity

Work together to investigate the history of clocks and how they are made.

Treat

Thumbprint cookies

Promptings

Watch or Read

"Helping Others Recognize the Whisperings of the Spirit," Sister Vicki F. Matsumori, October 2009 general conference (video and text available at lds.org)

Discuss

What is the role of the Holy Ghost in the Godhead? What is His purpose in the life of each of Heavenly Father's children? Why is the influence of the Holy Ghost so critical in the Church and in the world? How have you learned to recognize the promptings of the Spirit?

According to Sister Matsumori, how can we assist others in recognizing the still, small voice of the Spirit? How can we provide an atmosphere where we and our loved ones can more easily receive personal revelation?

President Thomas S. Monson has told us not to postpone acting on a prompting. How have you taken his counsel to heart?

Share personal experiences with the promptings of the Spirit, noting the many ways the Lord communicates with each of you. Choose something to focus on for the coming week that you feel will open your own heart to better communication with the Spirit.

Activity

Write your testimony for your spouse, then exchange and read them.

Treat

Sunshine cake

Provident Living

Watch or Read

"Becoming Provident Providers Temporally and Spiritually," Elder Robert D. Hales, April 2009 general conference (video and text available on lds.org)

Discuss

Talk about some of the reasons Heavenly Father has asked us to stay out of debt. What negative consequences can it have in our lives?

Because of our agency, we can choose what we do and become in this life. The Lord and His prophets have counseled us to avoid anything that will impair our judgment or otherwise restrict our ability to make wise choices. The more we bind up our lives with things that do not bring peace and happiness, the more we lose the ability to feel the Spirit of God.

What blessings have come to you as a result of paying your tithing? Do you currently view tithing as a blessing or a burden?

Recall different periods of your life, as Elder Hale did, where you learned different lessons about money and other things that can bind up our freedom. Why is it important to manage and budget your income? Why must "needful" things be placed before other wants and desires?

What experiences have you each had with budgeting and money management? What advice have you given to your children or other people you love?

What methods and solutions has the Lord provided to help us regain our peace and freedom if we are under the burden of debt?

Activity

Work on your budget together.

Treat

Penny candy

Race of Life

Watch or Read

"The Race of Life," President Thomas S. Monson, April 2012 general conference (video and text available at lds.org)

Discuss

Talk about a memorable trip you have taken as a couple or family. What was the purpose of the trip? How did you prepare? Did everything go the way you had planned? How did it feel to come home again?

Now, discuss mortal life, which the Apostle Paul likened to a race. Why did we choose to leave Heavenly Father's presence and experience mortality? How do you think we prepared? What do we need to accomplish here in order to return home to Him again? Talk about the blessings of knowing who we are, why we are here, and where we can go if we keep the commandments.

President Monson declared: "Although we come into mortality 'trailing clouds of glory,' life moves relentlessly forward. Youth follows childhood, and maturity comes ever so imperceptibly. From experience we learn the need to reach heavenward for assistance as we make our way along life's pathway."

How does Heavenly Father guide us on our eternal voyage? What means has He provided to ensure a safe return?

Activity

Make simple toy boats, then race them.

Treat

Root beer floats

Regrets

Watch or Read

"Of Regrets and Resolutions," President Dieter F. Uchtdorf, October 2012 general conference (video and text available on lds.org)

Discuss

What would you like to be known for at the end of your mortal life? From your experiences growing up, what memories made you want to be more like your parents or other close relatives? What did you learn from them that made you want to do better?

Discuss the resolutions President Uchtdorf challenged us to make in order to avoid regret.

- Resolve to spend more time with those we love.
- Resolve to strive more earnestly to become the person God wants us to be.
- Resolve to find happiness, regardless of your circumstances.

What improvements can be made in your own lives?

Activity

Go on a bike ride together.

Treat

Have dessert for dinner.

Repentance

Watch or Read

"Repent . . . That I May Heal You," Elder Neil L. Andersen, October 2009 general conference (video and text available on lds.org)

Discuss

Talk about Elder Andersen's statement that "When we sin, we turn away from God. When we repent, we turn back toward God."

Work together, using your scriptures, to create a definition of sin. What is it? How does it affect our relationship with ourselves, others, and our Heavenly Father?

Heavenly Father does not gain pleasure from watching His children struggle or from pointing out their sins to them. Instead, He asks us to put away things that keep us from feeling His love and keeping His commandments. As we read in Moses 3:19, His work and His glory is to bring to pass our immortality and eternal life.

Discuss the places each of you likes to go to feel loved and safe. Why do these places bring such comfort?

Review the following quote from Elder Andersen: "The scriptures speak of His arms begin open, extended, stretched out, and encircling. They are described as mighty and holy, arms of mercy, arms of safety, arms of love, 'lengthened out all the day long.'"

The Savior desires that we seek Him out during our times of trial as well as our joyful moments. He understands the pain and difficulties each of us faces, and He offers us love, comfort, and forgiveness. We can learn to single out His voice from all the others and turn toward Him.

What other voices and obstacles might block our way when we try to repent and turn back toward Christ? Discuss the influence of friends, media, personal expectations, and loss of self-worth on an individual's ability to repent and return to God.

Activity

Resolve to hug your spouse with complete love at least three times a day, beginning with the current moment.

Treat

Apple or cherry turnovers

Resolve

Watch or Read

"We Are Doing a Great Work and Cannot Come Down," President Dieter F. Uchtdorf, April 2009 general conference (video and text available on lds.org)

Discuss

Together with your spouse, prepare a short list of the things you consider most important in your lives. Items might include family, the gospel, work, hobbies, etc. Then, write down everything you did today. How many of the items from the day's activities were directly related to the things you said mattered most to you? Which things crept into the day that took time or attention away from what you wanted to be doing?

Recall President Uchtdorf's stories about the light bulb and Nehemiah. Discuss why it is so important to focus on keeping the commandments. How can Satan distract us, and what defenses do we have against his tactics? What adjustments can you make, together and individually, that will help build your defenses?

Activity

Work on your schedule and calendar together, making sure to allow for the things that matter most to you.

Treat

Monkey bread (represents a wall of defenses)

Respect

Watch or Read

"Respect and Reverence," Sister Margaret S. Lifferth, April 2009 general conference (video and text available on lds.org)

Discuss

Talk about Sister Lifferth's statement, "Respect for others and reverence for God are close cousins. They are rooted in humility and love . . . Elder L. Tom Perry taught that 'reverence flows from our admiration and respect for Deity.'"

How does our respect for others, or lack thereof, demonstrate how we feel about our Heavenly Father and our Savior Jesus Christ? How does the language we use in speaking of and to God affect the people around us? Does our home provide an atmosphere where others can learn reverence for Deity?

Discuss how you and your spouse can increase your reverence and respect for Church leaders, whether they are General Authorities or stake and local leaders. How can you show respect for everyone in your life, whether or not they are members of the Church?

Discuss specific situations in which paying closer attention and acting with respect will promote greater peace for you as individuals and your children and grandchildren.

Activity

Write thank-you notes to each other.

Treat

Bird's nest cookies

Restoration

Watch or Read

"Joseph Smith—Prophet of the Restoration," Elder Tad R. Callister, October 2009 general conference (video and text available on lds.org)

Discuss

Review Elder Callister's comparison of the gospel of Jesus Christ with a jigsaw puzzle. Discuss some of the truths we have because the Church was restored, and how our lives might be different without this knowledge. Review and discuss the four main points Elder Callister mentions in his address:

- God the Father and His Son, Jesus Christ, are two separate, distinct beings.
- The Father and Son have glorified bodies of flesh and bones.
- God still speaks to man.
- The full and complete gospel of Jesus Christ was not on the earth at the time when the First Vision occurred.

Discuss Joseph Smith's willingness to learn, ask, and follow through with each new piece of knowledge he received. His calling didn't make him less human or less prone to trials, but his righteous choices blessed many lives.

Because of the Prophet Joseph Smith, we know the answers to life's most important questions—what we need to do to become like Jesus and return to live with Heavenly Father. However, it is still up to each of us to learn about and fit each of those pieces into our hearts and lives. As we grow in the gospel, we gain access to more and more tools, or puzzle pieces, that we need to build a happy life and complete Heavenly Father's vision for us.

Tell each other about the newest piece of testimony you've added to your personal puzzle.

Activity

Complete a puzzle together.

Treat

Johnny cakes and honey

Righteous Judgment

Watch or Read

"Developing Good Judgment and Not Judging Others," Elder Gregory A. Schwitzer, April 2010 general conference (video and text available on lds.org)

Discuss

Open a box of chocolates. Without looking, choose one. Can you guess what flavor it is likely to be? Talk about the different ways there are to judge things around us. Why is it important to use all of our senses and abilities to problem-solve when making a decision?

Discuss other types of situations where decisions need to be made. What would happen if one of your children or grandchildren, or a niece or nephew, didn't take time to consider consequences before making an important decision? For example, he or she might quickly choose to be friends with someone based on the fact that the person lives nearby, or is physically attractive, without considering whether or not they had similar values and interests, were of similar ages, etc.

Review the story of Mary and Martha. Was one sister better than the other? What information would we need in order to make a correct judgment? Emphasize that only the Savior really knew the entire story. Similarly, with all the people we know now, only Jesus Christ and our Heavenly Father know their hearts.

Remember that while we must make judgments or decisions on a daily basis, we have been commanded not to condemn one another, but to "judge righteous judgment" (John 7:24).

Heavenly Father has given us many tools to help us make good decisions. Take a moment to review and discuss four tools Elder Schwitzer identifies. Apply these principles to help you better understand your spouse.

Activity

Play "The Rest of the Story." Begin telling your companion a story about your youth and then let him or her finish it for you any way he or she wants before you share the real ending to the story. Reverse rolls, and continue to share stories from your past.

Treat

Share a couple of chocolates.

Scripture Study

Watch or Read

"The Blessing of Scripture," Elder D. Todd Christofferson, April 2010 general conference (video and text available on lds.org)

Discuss

What is your favorite verse of scripture? What feelings does it invoke when you turn to that page in your scriptures or find the verse on your electronic device?

Discuss how Heavenly Father helped people accomplish difficult things so that we could have the scriptures. Why is it so important for us to read and study what is written in them?

Does the Lord expect us to make great sacrifices as Nephi, Joseph Smith, William Tyndale, and others did? What kinds of sacrifices do we need to make in order to honor theirs?

The scriptures help us understand the gospel of Jesus Christ. They bring us comfort and peace. They teach us what to do and what not to do. The scriptures teach us to repent, serve others, make sacred covenants, and follow the example of Jesus Christ.

The men who sacrificed to bring us the words of the Lord have given us a priceless gift. We show our gratitude by valuing the scriptures as much as they did and by making them a part of our daily lives. If we aren't reading and studying the scriptures, we lose an opportunity to draw closer to our Heavenly Father and our Savior. How does Elder Christofferson illustrate this point?

Activity

Play Scripture Pictionary. Draw pictures of your favorite scripture stories and see how long it takes your partner to guess the stories.

Treat

Use the internet to find a recipe for scripture-based cookies, where the ingredients are "hidden" in scripture verses. Then make the cookies.

Service

Watch or Read

"Finding Joy through Loving Service," Elder M. Russell Ballard, April 2011 general conference (video and text available on lds.org)

Discuss

Review Elder Ballard's story of a young prospector during the California Gold Rush. What was the difference between the reaction of the young man and the reaction of the older prospector who also found gold? How did each of them seem to feel about it?

Elder Ballard explains the importance of developing Christlike love for those around us, and of providing service—or active love—to them. When we focus on service, we fill our souls with spiritual gold and help fill other people's pouches. What does Elder Ballard say about the size or magnitude of our acts of service?

Address the three areas of opportunity for service: home, church, and community. Discuss how service can be given in small and simple ways. Is the service we give in each of these areas similar or different? How do we use our different personalities and talents to give that service?

Activity

Donate blood together.

Treat

Mini chocolate bars

Small and Simple Things

Watch or Read

"Let Him Do It with Simplicity," Elder L. Tom Perry, October 2008 general conference (video and text available on lds.org)

Discuss

Discuss the impact of seemingly small promptings, choices, and actions in our lives. How do little acts of kindness, love, and understanding help build great marriages?

Has there been a "Walden Pond" period in your life? What did you give up and simplify in order to focus on the simplest needs and priorities? If you were to plan for such an event in your life, what would the details be?

What is one small aspect of this dream that you could follow in the here and now? Are you overlooking ways of bringing greater peace into your life through the art of simplicity?

Discuss and express gratitude for the ways in which your needs in life have been met.

Activity

Schedule and plan a "jammie day" with your spouse. Plan on a relaxing, stress-free day, free of electronic devices. Begin with breakfast in bed and lounge around in your pajamas, simply enjoying each other's company for the day.

Treat

Design your own cornucopia of fresh fruits and vegetables to eat for dinner while remembering your blessings.

Stories of Jesus

Watch or Read

"Tell Me the Stories of Jesus," Elder Neil L. Andersen, April 2010 general conference (video and text available on lds.org)

Discuss

Darken the room as much as possible, then light a single candle. Talk about all the things the flame can represent—beauty, warmth, light, etc. Would the candle give enough light to help you walk through the room? Discuss the difference multiple candles can make to the darkness in a room and for a person's confidence if they needed to use that light to find their way.

Jesus Christ is the Light of the World. He is the Way that leads to eternal life. We look to Him in order to find our path through the trials of mortality. He has asked us to nurture the flame of our testimonies and to use that light to help others. However, we cannot depend on another person's light for direction and strength to make it back to

Heavenly Father. Only our own testimony, and the Lord's light, can sufficiently light our way.

Discuss the reasons it is so important to learn all that we can about Jesus Christ. Look through the *Gospel Art Book* together, pointing out additional stories and life lessons that can be obtained from them as shown in the examples from Elder Andersen's talk.

Activity

Have a read-a-thon for the book of John.

Treat

Loaves and fishes: make open-face tuna melt sandwiches with English muffins, tuna salad, and cheese slices. Warm the second half of the English muffin to eat with butter and honey for dessert.

Temples

Watch or Read

"Temple Mirrors of Eternity: A Testimony of Family," Elder Gerrit W. Gong, October 2010 general conference (video and text available on lds.org)

Discuss

Talk about why eternal families and temple work are so important in Heavenly Father's plan. How do temple ordinances serve not just the central family unit, but all the generations of a family?

Discuss the need for temple worthiness in our everyday lives. What standards do we need to live up to in order to attend the temple? Why are these standards necessary?

Only through repentance and reliance on the Atonement can we enter Heavenly Father's house. The Atonement is also key to the covenants we make in the temple. An eternal family is created as each member chooses to place Jesus Christ at the center of his or her life.

When we look into a single mirror we can see only ourselves. The mirrors of the temple offer us a different perspective, one that is eternal and all encompassing.

Activity

Go to the temple together. Spend time walking the grounds if you are unable to go inside.

Treat

Pineapple

Testimony

Read

Matthew 25

Discuss

How does having a testimony of Jesus Christ change how we live our lives? Recall and share the beginnings of your own testimonies.

Consider why one sacrament meeting per month is dedicated to bearing testimony. How does having a testimony of Jesus Christ change how we live our lives? Is gaining a testimony an isolated event or an ongoing process? What is the difference between having a testimony and being converted?

Talk about ways to fill your spiritual lamp with oil. How can a person strengthen his or her testimony and be more converted? Discuss whether each suggestion feels like a major effort (taking the missionary discussions and being baptized) or a small effort (remembering nighttime prayers). Remember that little things are often done with much more regularity and therefore can add up to a bigger portion of oil. Large and small, every effort toward learning and growth counts.

Similarly, how can you strengthen your relationship with your spouse? Why do you think the Savior used a marriage celebration to symbolize the joy of eternal life?

Activity

Create a simple massage oil from a recipe on the internet, then give each other a massage.

Treat

Wedding cookies

About the Author

Alison Palmer is a life-long member of the LDS Church who delights in finding ways to inspire a love of the gospel and joyful living in others. You can usually find her hiding in her home office or lurking in any bookstore or library she can find. If she's not there, she might be playing with her children and grandchildren, playing piano, taking long naps, or cooking things that have far more calories than nutritional merits.

Alison is the author of nearly a dozen gospel-centered books, including *A Companion to the Children's Songbook* and *Family Night Lessons to Prepare Your Child for Baptism.*